Pit of Despair

Pit of Despair

UROOSA KASHIF

Woven Words Publishers OPC Pvt. Ltd.

Registered Office:

Vill: Raipur, P.O: Raipur Paschimbar,

Dist: Purba Midnapore, Pin: 721401,

West Bengal, India.

Branch Office(Operations): Hyderabad

www.wovenwordspublishers.com

Email: publish@wovenwordspublishers.com

First published by Woven Words Publishers OPC Pvt. Ltd., 2018

NONFICTION

IMPRINT: WOVEN WORDS NONFICTION

ISBN 13: 978-93-86897-48-0

ISBN 10: 93-86897-48-2

Price: $ 5/₹100

Printed and bound in India by Woven Words Publishers.

Printed and bound in US by Amazon.

Part 1

Chapter: 1

I was on a call when it happened; I was talking to my mother about something pleasant. I don't recall what it was but we were laughing, I was about to say something when I felt like someone grabbed my neck, the next second I found myself almost choking, drowning in a deep misery. I did not know what I was grieving about but the sadness was so profound, that I had to disconnect the call at once to find out what was happening.

I called my maid to get me a glass of cold water, and as soon as I took a sip I broke down in tears and for hours I sat at the same spot in the same sofa, crying, without even realizing that the day has changed. I felt like everyone I know is dead and the world around me has come to an end, there began the darkest period of my life.

That was not the first depression attack I encountered, I had several before that. When you have depression you have it for years or months, it doesn't come or go in days. With me it was happening for seven years more or less, but that night was the first time I realized that it is out of my hands now and I will have to get help for it, seriously.

Chapter 2:

Recognizing depression as an illness:

From where I come, people care about each other according to their own convenience.

Say if I am having seasonal flu, or a mild case of stomach disorder I will find myself surrounded by my friends, gasping in concern and offering condolences and comforts. My family will come with worrisome faces and fruit baskets to make sure I'm well fed and not physically weak. But none of them will offer any comfort if I am diagnosed with a mental disorder, understanding about someone's mental health is a lot of effort and it simply doesn't suit the traditional south Asian family cut outs.

I specifically remember that after my C-section, my family came to see me in hospital, they did what not to comfort me but when I told them about my depression they did not seem to understand what I said. It was like I spoke in some alien language. My aunt specifically said, "esa kuch nai hota" (there's no such thing as depression). It's not like they were not acquainted with the term or they couldn't hear about it, they used this word quite often in day to day language, they just didn't take it as an illness, in South Asian families, no one wants to know about it, no one wants to hear about it but more than everything no one wants to say that it's inherited, it was a shame for them to accept that the disease has lingered in the family tree for generations, and off course this depressed me more that no one was actually giving any consideration to my medical condition and that was the biggest obstacle I faced in getting help from a psychiatrist.

Discussing mental health issue was a subject most taboo, I, myself was in denial for years because I hailed from the same society, for me it mattered that people don't brand me insane because I have a mental illness I didn't seek help from a professional psychiatrist for years, I had run a family and a business and it was only possible when I made people believe that I'm capable of taking care of them all.

I remembered reading about someone online that she had borderline split personality disorder, and her mother accused her that she is making stuff up just to get attention, so many cases are there where patients actually die, they commit suicide because of the stress but the parents or guardian never pay any attention to what was going on in their patients head.

Though my life seemed remarkably meaningless, I was not sick enough going to throw myself off a cliff, luckily I had some sense left in me which made me think of a rational way out of it all. I read. I used to spend hours reading stories of how people dealt with it, what helped them coming out of depression and what them more depressed and there I found out about an online community of depression patients which was formed to help others like me to get an idea of this plague has been affecting other lives too. It was comforting to know that I wasn't alone and that there are others who are going through the same; like my mother quoted I wasn't doing it to get attention after all.

Being a part of that online community wasn't very pleasant on everyday basis and some days I had ended up feeling more depressed than I actually was, there were those who were mourning the deaths of their young kids, those who were drug addicts and even those who have killed other people either by accident or will but there was one thing in common in all of us, everyone had a family to live for, and no one was ready to give up life because of this disease. Our battles were hard and different, but we all wanted to live.

People proposed different sorts of drug free methods to overcome depression, since I couldn't consult a psychiatrist I started scrolling through other patients suggestions, some opted for pets, some began to paint, there was someone from turkey who said he began writing journal and that clicked my attention, same day I read about journaling I bought a diary and penned my first entry.

It read "I want to climb out of my pit of despair."

Chapter3:

Accepting that I needed professional help:

Strong women find it very hard to accept that they have a weakness; let it be an illness or a shortcoming, as I told I had to raise a family and run a business it was daunting for me to let people know about my mental health. Luckily My kids were way young to notice any change in my behavior, as long as I was smiling they couldn't know what was going in my mind and that was a blessing and no matter how much was I depressed I never took it out on my surroundings so my immediate family was safe from the effects of illness. In my appearance or conduct I never looked like a lunatic, I performed better than those who had a sane mind in almost every department of life. I was a caring mother and a caring wife, no one would've guessed what was going on in my head so convince my husband and family was the biggest obstacle I faced first.

So I began to light.

When I first told my husband that I'm always sad about something or the other he suggested that I should take a break from the office. "You should try the regular housewife stuff, watch serial, read a book, sleep, spend time with the infant, you'll be fine". He thought that I'm overworked, so, I took a break of a few days and didn't go to the office at all but sitting home only worsened the condition. I was vacant and depressed and was crying in showers for long so I rejoined work, for a few days I was fine but again the deep grief began kicking in, I was still sick.

Then one night, during a dinner I told him clearly how I feel; he looked concerned and blamed himself for this. According to him, he was the reason I was continuously sad, but I convinced him that this is not how it works. By the end of the night, I succeeded to convince him to take me to a psychiatrist coming Saturday.

Part 2

Chapter 4:

What is Depression?

The Diagnostic and Statistical Manual of Mental Disorders classifies depression into the following basic types:

Dysthymia: In essence, having a depressed mood on most days for at least two years.

Major Depressive Disorder: In addition to feeling "down" as in dysthymia, other characteristics may include excessive feelings of remorse and suicidal ideation, as well as various physical symptoms like loss of appetite and fatigue. It can be mild, moderate, or severe.

Adjustment disorder: With Depressed Mood, this is grief due to a loss of some kind. Depression NOS (not otherwise specified). Includes things like premenstrual depression and seasonal depression (SAD). Secondary depression. Depression due to an underlying medical disorder like Cushing's disease or hypothyroidism. Though not in DSM-IV, some practitioners further classify depression into two broad types: Endogenous (or chemical) depression to denote depression that arises without an obvious identifiable cause, thought to reflect some kind of "chemical imbalance" in the brain. Exogenous (or external) depression which is thought to arise from a specific, identifiable external cause. Given this confusing and non-parallel classification scheme, it is astonishing doctors do not become depressed themselves as they try to figure out into which bucket their patient's depression fits!

How can we make sense of all this and, more importantly, understand the real cause of depression in order to augment the effectiveness of currently available therapies? Depression is a common but serious medical illness that negatively affects how one feels; the way one thinks and how one acts. It causes a feeling of sadness and/or loss of interest in activities one enjoyed once; it can lead to a variety of physical and emotional problems and can decrease a person's ability to function at work or in the home.

Depression is a strange road between truth and fiction:

Those who have depression tend to see the reality more. This goes both ways, against and in favour, how? While you are stripping away the layers of illusion to find the worst in every situation, you come across the best in every situation too. In my case, there were days when I thought no one actually cared what I wanted for my life and there surfaced the faces of parents and brothers who actually did the world to make me happy.

My best friend couldn't set the art gallery he always dreamed of, but at least his company was good enough to pay 30 people their salaries. He was providing a lot of people a reason to get up and go on with their lives, more than that he was indirectly he was making sure that the families of his employees don't sleep empty stomach.

This is how it works, every time you will think of something bad something good will come up to you and this will keep you going.

Depression is the fastest growing mental illness in Pakistan:

Pakistan Medical Association on Thursday said that the depression in the country was much higher than the worlds average while its incidence was alarmingly high in big cities, declaring depression as the theme on the world health day this year PMA said that the mental issues were mainly growing in the cities. Around 35.7 per cent of citizens of Karachi are affected while 43 per cent people in Quetta, 53.4 per cent in Lahore said Dr Qaisar Sajjad Secretary Gen of PMA. Where globally it affected 20 per cent in Pakistan it was 34 per cent.

Part 3

Treat yourself

Are you in a rut?

You keep doing something just because you have done it for long:

I wanted to study literature, instead I was brainwashed to study accounts, it was very hard for me to finish the program but I did it anyhow, after I completed my ACCA, I went out to have a job and couldn't work for long as an accountant because I didn't feel happy there but because I have invested five long years in finishing the program and one more year in the internship it was hard to change my career then. Day after day I became silent at work and stopped talking to people around me unless it was only about work. One day when I came home from the bank and I saw my dad sitting in our garden, he asked me why do I look so tired and I said I don't feel like doing this job. So don't do it he simply said. He asked me what I feel like doing, and I told him I wanted to write and within a few days, he arranged my visa and tickets to attend this writing workshop in the US. I opted to change my career because I did not want to keep doing something I didn't like just because I had done it for years.

If it costs you your peace it's too expensive.

You are waiting for a miracle to happen:

Say you have been chasing a boy/girl who does not stand the sight of your face or cringes when he/she hears your name, you won't make him or her fall in love with you no matter what you try, you are dreaming for impossible, stop. Stop putting efforts on people or things you can't possibly have. This is the most common reason in teen to fall in a rut, you keep calling someone u cannot have, you keep thinking about someone else's wife or husband, stop trying to win them over, value those who are near you.

The 50-50 situation: Longer work hours at a harder job may land you the promotion, but then again, it may not. And in the meantime, you may get stressed out.

Ditch the dead-end. Don't go near a dead end. When caught in a negative situation, small positive cues may signal that things will improve eventually when in fact they may not. Instead of remaining in a dead-end situation, determine objectively whether things are improving overall.

Regret is natural:

Regret may paralyse you from making progress, but studies show that *counterfactual thinking* can actually help motivate you to act. Counterfactual thinking is the process of constructively assessing how something might have happened, asking the question, "What might I have done?" It prompts a new and empowering resolve: *"When X happens (or doesn't happen), I will do Y."*

There are two kinds of counterfactual thinking, and only one of them has positive benefits. For example, say you are stuck because you did not get the job you wanted. You could employ *downward counterfactual thinking*—"Well, it could have been worse. At least I got the interview"—but this will not induce any progress. The positive alternative is to try *counterfactual thinking* upward—imagining a better alternative that allows you to see how you might have acted or reacted to seek solutions. While mentally reviewing the interview, you realize that you could have been more forthcoming. So you modify your future interview behaviour and get a job offer.

Get out of your comfort zone, challenge yourself:

To get out of your rut, understand what keeps you *in* it. You may be caught in your comfort zone, a situation that feels familiar because of your early childhood experience. Those that grew up in loving and supportive families rarely find themselves in a negative rut. Those who grew up in harmful emotional environments, however, may have a comfort zone that feels familiar but is still harmful. When trying to move past a negative situation, ask yourself: Does an aspect of this situation seem familiar? Learn where your responses are coming from is a first step toward getting yourself on the move.

Set realistic targets:

Sometimes we can be overwhelmed by the amount of change required to get out of a rut, and that keeps us in it. To solve this, set manageable interim goals.

Be mindful that we tend to exaggerate our abilities or wrongly attribute failure to circumstances beyond our control. Be ruthlessly realistic about how your talents match up with the goal you set. If your goal seems unreachable, pull back and master *mental contrasting*.

I AM ENOUGH.
WHO I AM IS
ENOUGH.
WHAT I DO
IS ENOUGH,
AND WHAT I HAVE
IS ENOUGH.

Indulge, dwell:

Mental contrasting helps you stay motivated by that desired future while keeping you realistic about the steps needed to fix hindrances. To do it, contemplate your ideal future *while* thinking about the short-term factors that stand in the way of achieving it. Just imagining the future alone (*indulging*) or thinking about the possible problems alone (*dwelling*) will not propel you into meaningful action and can actually leave you stuck.

Faith and belief may help, or they may not:

I've already told how much of our thinking isn't as deliberate as we think. We are all vulnerable to *cognitive distortions*, one of which is a combination of magical logic and misattribution of cause and effect. B.F. Skinner described it in a study he called "Superstition in the Pigeon." (I do not endorse animal cruelty.) Skinner put very, very hungry pigeons in cages and swung a food dish into the cages at random intervals. When the pigeons got hungry again, 75% of the birds would repeat whatever they were doing when the food arrived. They attributed to cause and effect to whatever action—such as hopping on one foot or flapping their wings—"made" the food appears the last time. People do that, too. Something good happens, and you attribute it to the prayer you uttered, the candle you lit, or the lucky shirt you wore. To get out of the rut, stop inferring cause and effect like Skinner's superstitious pigeon. It will just keep you on the hamster wheel even longer.

Fill out the following and conclude, for a sample, I am filling the first tab.

Major Activities	Things I do	Things I say	Things I do not do	Things I want to do	Things others made me do/say
Morning routine	I always get up for prayers, and that is 5 a.m.	Wish mornings, give instructions to my family about getting up and go on with the day	Don't sit properly to eat breakfast, don't pack the lunchbox for myself. Don't kiss my son goodbye. Don't check on my birds in the morning.	Sleep for a few more minutes. Few more minutes in the shower. Lemon juice, not coffee.	I prayed because my mother in law said so. Left for office early because my employees wanted me in the office early.

Shopping trends					
Meals					
Conversation starters					
Travelling preferences					
Comfort zones at work					
Driving trends					
Night Routine					
What's on my mind/ what was I thinking all day?					
How creative					

was I?					

Chapter: Talk.

My psychiatrist who actually became a very good friend later wrote this on my prescription the first day "You are alienated from a social life form because of why depression is kicking in, talk to people". It was ridiculous, and I was almost angry at her stating so, especially when I clearly told her about my routine. I used to go to a 20 people office, I was supposed to talk to at least 10 of them on a daily basis, I hailed from a joint family so I was in conversation with my mother in law too, my maids and a driver was there in my house to speak to, and above all my husband and kids were always telling me about something or the other. I could not make sense of my doctor's diagnosis unless she asked me to write in the journal what I spoke daily. She asked me to count my sentences along the day and circle all the repetitive words, it sounded like a grammar exercise at first but when I read what I spoke during the day I realized that I was either giving instructions or taking orders. Nowhere in the day had an actual meaningful conversation happened.

Person to talk to	What to say to them and why	What will you achieve after the conversation
Best friend		
Mother	Talk about your childhood; the early years are usually pleasant, parents and family is enthusiastic to raise you, you don't do anything but eat and sleep, your farts are funny and smiles are adorable, everyone loves you. If this isn't the case with you and you have an unlucky childhood, find something to talk about.	Talking about your childhood will make you feel like there were some happy years in your life, you will want to relive those days to whatever extent possible, forgetting about the current disaster.
Father	Ask them how difficult was it for him to raise you because it sure was difficult. Fathers are misunderstood figures, most of the kids do not open up to their	You will realize that every time you thought you were left alone, or no one cared about you, your dad was the one who was secretly worried about you, then

	fathers because they think their dad might not get it, but it's wrong. Remember, someone was working day and night because your football coaching was expensive, or piano lessons were ridiculously costly, that guy deserved to be appreciated for all the overtime he had done at the office.	you will know that there is someone who still worries about you and for whom you have to get up and get better.
School friend	School is where the fun happens, call a childhood friend if you can or use social media connecting sites to get in touch with them. Search for any photos of your childhood, you will feel rejuvenated.	It has always worked in my case. I used to call my childhood friend whenever I was down and she used to gossip with for hours about unnecessary things just to keep me from sadness. It can work on your case too.
Grandparents	If they're alive no one on earth has loved you more.	Go cuddle them even if they're not well, there a scent resides in

		old people's clothes which makes you feel secure. Try it on my request, it works.
kids	They're the other face of God, they are honest they are true they are imaginative, they are kind, they are loving and very expressive which is very good. Learn how they find goodness in everything, how are they excited about even little things, how it hurts them when their friends are not talking to them and above all how they express themselves every time they love something or hate something.	My son wanted to learn calligraphy, yes, at the age of four! So I arranged a tutor, he used to write with his left hand(still does) and it was challenging for him to draw curves without tilting a little forward, but he realised that he had to overcome it, so he used to get up in the nights to practice. This immensely inspired me; I knew that I had to try as hard as him to overcome my weakness. Let your kids be your inspiration to overcome depression.
Husband/boyfriend		

Wife /girlfriend		
Teachers/mentors		
Siblings/cousins		

Chapter: Cry:

While the sheer frustration of lousy day at work could make me cry, once I could wipe my tears away the world could seem like it's been put back together again. I found out in my sessions that tears could be a way of flushing negative chemicals out of the system. A study by Dr William H Frey a biochemist at St. Paul Ramsey medical centre in Minnesota found that there is a difference between a tear caused by mental stress and a tear caused by physical/non-emotional reason like cutting onion, emotional tear contain more of protein-based hormone which is produced by our body when we are stressed, 88.8 per cent of people feel better after a good cry so breaking the stereotype I began crying whenever I felt like it, and it helped.

"Life isn't about

waiting for the

storm to pass, it's

about learning

how to dance in

the rain."

— Author Unknown

Chapter: Figure out why you hold it all in.
Now that you know all the good things that come
about when you cry think about what might be
stopping your tears from flowing. If it has been a
long time since you have been able to cry, you may
need to make a conscious effort to get to the point
where you can release your emotions through tears.
Do you harbour negative thoughts about crying? If
so, try to change your views and see that there's
nothing wrong with crying - it is good for you. Do
you have trouble expressing feelings in general?

Allowing yourself to cry will be a good start for you. Being able to process emotions in this way will help you be more emotional in general.

When you push your feelings down and keep yourself from crying, those feelings do not go away. You may feel either angry or numb. When you're finished crying, think about how you feel. If you're like most people, you will find that your brain feels a bit freer of the emotion that was bogging you down. You might not feel joyful right away, but you probably feel calmer, less anxious, and ready to take on your problems. Hold onto that feeling, and get into the habit of crying when you need to. It'll get easier with practice.

According to one study, 85% of women report feeling better after crying, while 73% of men do. If you do not feel good after crying, consider why. It can be hard to shake off years of being told that crying is weak, and so on. If you are embarrassed that you cried, try to remember that it's completely natural and healthy.

Avoid alcohol or other forms of drugs:

The downside is that it can make you unfit to drive, to operate machinery and affects your ability to make decisions. It also dulls your perception to a greater or less extent, depending on the amount of alcohol consumed. If you go on drinking, your speech starts to slur, you become unsteady on your feet and may start to say things you may regret the next day. If you drink, even more, most people start to feel sleepy, sick or dizzy. You may pass out. The next day you may be unable to remember what happened while you were drinking. Alcohol can be a very effective way of feeling better for a few hours. If you are depressed and lacking in energy, it can be tempting to use alcohol to help you keep going and cope with life. The problem is that it is easy to slip into regularly drinking, using it as a medication. The benefits soon wear off, and the drinking becomes part of a routine. You start to notice that:

- Instead of *choosing* to have a drink, you *feel* you have to have it, you wake up with shaky hands and a feeling of nervousness, you start to drink earlier and earlier, your work starts to suffer, your drinking starts to affect your relationships, you carry on drinking despite the problems it causes, you find you have to drink more and more to get the same effect (tolerance), you start to 'binge drink' (see below) regularly, other things have less importance than alcohol. Psychosis - hearing voices when there is nobody there dementia - memory loss, rather like Alzheimer's dementia physical - damage organs, such as the liver or brain.

We know that there is a connection – self-harm and suicides are much more common in people with alcohol problems. It seems that it can work in two ways: you regularly drink too much including (including 'binge drinking') which makes you feel depressed or you drink to relieve anxiety or depression.

Either way, Alcohol affects the chemistry of the brain, increasing the risk of depression. Hangovers can create a cycle of waking up feeling ill, anxious, jittery and guilty. Life gets depressing – arguments with family or friends, trouble at work, memory and sexual problems.

Some drinks are stronger than others. The easiest way to work out how much you are drinking is to count the 'units' of alcohol in your drinks. 1 unit is 8 grams /10 ml of pure alcohol - the amount in a standard 25 ml measure of spirits, a half pint of 3.6% beer or lager, or a 100 ml glass of 12% wine (see table below).

If a man and woman of the same weight drink the same amount of alcohol, the woman will end up with a much higher amount in the organs of her body. So the safe limit is lower for women (14 units per week) than for men (21 units per week).

Young people in the UK drink to have fun, to have the experience of losing control, to socialise more easily with others, to feel sexier – and because their friends do. Around a third of 15-16-year-olds binge-drink three or more times a month - more than in most other European countries. Alcohol seems to have the same depressant effect in younger people as it does in adults. Around a third of young suicides have drunk alcohol before their death, and increased drinking may have been to blame for the rising rates of teenage male suicide.

As we get older, we tend to lose muscle and to put on fat. Alcohol isn't absorbed by fat, so it ends up in the non-fatty tissues of the body. So, an older person who is the same weight as a younger person will tend to have more alcohol in their vital organs (non-fatty tissues) such as brain, muscles and liver. This means that alcohol will affect an older person more.

The published weekly safe limits assume that you spread your drinking out with at least two alcohol-free days per week. This may not be the case – you drink a lot in one night, but remain within your 'safe' limit if you do not drink for the rest of the week. There is evidence that even a couple of days of heavy drinking can start to kill off brain cells, as happens with people who drink continuously. Drinking over eight units in a day for men, or 6 units for women is known as binge drinking. In any one day, it is best for a man to drink no more than 3-4 units and for a woman to drink no more than 2-3 units.

Binge drinking also seems to be connected with an increased risk of early death in middle-aged men and probably depression.

Be associated with expressive art (in my case, I wrote).

Paint, sing, act, travel, write, make sculptures, make pots, do something creative. Put pen to paper and try to capture the essence of your feelings. You can start by writing down a description of the source of your emotions. Describe the ins and outs of your breakup, discuss the last few months of your father's illness, and write about how you lost your job at the start of the recession. Then go more in-depth and write about how that event has changed your life, and what you are feeling as a result. Writing down memories is also a good way to bring you to the point of tears.

Regulate your life. Clutter is half the depression:

day	week	month	year
read	movie	Charity	travel
Healthy Meals	School friend reunion	Social welfare	Go back hometown
Walk	Car cleaning	Room renovation	Go camping
Pets	De-clutter	Redecorating office	
Plants	Cook outside the house	Cook outside the house	
Meaningful			

conversations			
Avoid gadgets			
intimacy			

Exercise/meditate:

Exercise increases your overall health and your sense of well-being, which puts more pep in your step every day. But exercise also has some direct stress-busting benefits.

* **It pumps up your endorphins.** Physical activity helps to bump up the production of your brain's feel-good neurotransmitters, called endorphins. Although this function is often referred to as a runner's high, a rousing game of tennis or a nature hike also can contribute to this same feeling.
* **It's meditation in motion.** After a fast-paced game of racquetball or several laps in the pool, you will often find that you have forgotten the day's irritations and concentrated only on your body's movements.

  As you begin to shed your daily tensions through movement and physical activity regularly, you may find that this focus on a single task, and the resulting energy and optimism, can help you remain calm and clear in everything you do.

- **It improves your mood.** Regular exercise can increase self-confidence, it can relax you, and it can lower the symptoms associated with mild depression and anxiety. Exercise can also improve your sleep, which is often disrupted by stress, depression and anxiety. All of these exercise benefits can ease your stress levels and give you a sense of command over your body and your life.

Sleep:

Get depressed insomniac people to sleep, and their healing potentials doubles with mind being at a break from all the thinking. Depression currently is afflicting 30% of Americans, worldwide it is second to heart disease in economic cost, Biweekly CBT for insomnia over a month. Much of what was taught is fundamental human biology. You get people to go to sleep at the same time each night and get up at the same time each day; *move from the bed when not sleeping*; calm down and rest in the period before sleep. When people did these few active steps, they felt much better. Part of the CBT, honed over several decades of treating insomnia, was a simple principle—don't turn sleep into a job. When you make sleeping in a form of work, sleep does not work.

Why Would Sleep Therapies Be More Effective Than Other Depressive Treatments?

They tap into what happens with depression—a near total lack of adaptability and resilience. The body looks and acts like it is shutting down. Immunity does not respond well to new bacterial and viral threats. Appetitederails—going up or down, sideways, becoming erratic. Fatigue begins and deepens. Eventually, cognition—the ability to think, reason, solve problems—declines or plain disappears. Then people experience the misery of despair which cannot see its end. They feel that they will never get better, and there is nothing that will make them better in effect depression means normal physiological regeneration slowly shuts down. Sleep is required for many, many regenerative functions. Shut sleep down, and the organism does not function well—or eventually function at all. Deprive animals of sleep for long enough, and they die. However, get sleep up and running again and regeneration renews.

So How Is Sleep Related to Depression?

Poor sleep eventually results in depression. Professor Angst of the University of Zurich showed through decades of studies that the longer insomnia, the more confident the appearance of depression. Similarly, if people are becoming depressed—say as a result of hypothyroidism or a severe personal loss—their sleep declines in effectiveness and consistency. Make depression worse and sleep worsens. Make sleep difficult or inconsistent and depressive symptoms appear and increase.

What Does This Say About Prevention of Mood Disorders?

Why have American rates of depression doubled and tripled in the last half century? Hypotheses number in the dozens. However, this kind of study helps to argue that sleep loss—the 90 minutes we have cut off each night during the last forty years of American life—may have a necessary role to play in making the population more stressed—and ultimately more depressed. *Also, the same cognitive-behavioural principles of the timing of sleep, the timing of light, calm and rest before sleep, can be applied across the nation—to pretty much anyone who is not physically ill.*

The answer to health is proper regeneration. That also means recognising the body as an ever learning, adapting, the renewing system of information. Without proper sleep and regeneration, the system will break down—and depressive symptoms appear.

Also, now we know about that converse—that even nasty depressive episodes are treated more effectively if people are taught and trained to sleep—again effectively

Confide in a friend if you are comfortable with it. It can really help to talk to someone else about what made you sad, angry, or overwhelmed. Discuss your feelings until you have nothing left to talk about or cry about. You may even consider seeking help from a therapist if you find yourself needing to cry for extended periods of time. This may indicate a serious issue, such as unresolved grief or depression.

Find out the reason: About two years ago a fellow patient, Mrs Ahmad (not her real name), committed suicide. When her husband, who was also my patient, told me the news at one of his visits, I was shocked. Fully aware that 40% of older patients who are most likely to kill themselves visit their primary care doctors *within one week* of killing themselves, I found myself wondering over and over how I had missed recognising the severity of his distress. I had known he had been suffering from but had thought it mild.

However, even more, shocking than the news of his suicide was the reason his wife gave for it: six months earlier, he had been involved in a car accident and had inadvertently killed a pedestrian. In the end, he just couldn't live with the guilt.

Mind vs Brain:

First, we need to recognise the distinction between chemical and external depression has become outdated. Many neuroscientists have suggested that the mind arises from, and is caused by, the physical brain, meaning chemical and electrical reactions somehow give rise to thoughts and emotions. Evidence in support of this theory can be found in numerous studies that show altering brain chemistry with anti-depressant drugs (chemicals) can make depressed people feel better emotionally. The same is true for anxiolytics (like Valium) and their effect on anxiety.

But recently, with the advent of functional MRI scans (fMRI), we now have proof the opposite is equally true, that *changes in thinking* cause significant, measurable changes in brain chemistry and functioning. In one study, patients suffering from spider phobia underwent fMRI scanning before and after receiving cognitive behavioural therapy aimed at eliminating their fear of spiders. Scans were then compared to normal subjects without spider phobia. Results showed that brain function in patients with spider phobia before receiving cognitive behavioural therapy was abnormal compared to subjects without spider phobia but then *changed to match normal brain patterns after cognitive behavioural therapy*. This may represent the best evidence to date that changes made at the mind level can functionally "rewire" the brain, and that the brain and the mind are more mutually influential than we'd previously thought. It certainly supports the Buddhist view that brain and mind are only two sides of the same coin or different ways of viewing the same single thing.

Depression always has a cause:

Where, then, does the exact cause of depression lie? I would argue that depression arises at its core from *a belief that we are powerless to solve our problems.*

This is clearly true for people who know why they are depressed: invariably, once they figure out how to solve their particular problem, their depression lifts. However, I would also argue this holds true for people who are depressed for no reason they know. Why? Because thoughts can trigger feelings that remain stirred up *long after the thoughts themselves have been forgotten.* Some studies have suggested people think upwards of 12,000 thoughts per day. How could we ever remember them all? Yet a fleeting thought we might have had this morning about the possibility of losing our job can and often does leave an emotional residue that lasts hours, days, weeks, or even longer. I would argue; therefore, any depression that appears to be "chemical" is more likely caused by a thought that is merely *remembered*— thought about a problem we don't believe we can solve.

Further, sometimes what appears to be a "chemical" depression is caused by a thought that isn't directly or consciously *recognised*. These thoughts are often about problems that seem so unbearably awful and unsolvable we don't want (and often refuse) to think about them (such as our becoming jobless or the prospect of our death).

Finally, I believe the commonly accepted idea that chemical or hormonal abnormalities cause some forms of depression like depression NOS and secondary depression (#4 and #5 above) overstates the case. I would suggest an alternative explanation, which these forms of depression have a chemical or hormonal *influence—reducing* our ability to believe we can solve our problems but not eliminating it. At first glance, this might not appear to be a significant distinction given how incredibly difficult it is to believe in our ability to solve problems, for example, when experiencing premenstrual syndrome. However, knowing *intellectually* we can win even if we are having a hard time *believing* it can help to sustain the most valuable thing depression tends to reduce: hope.

How can you stand on your feet?

None of this is by any means to say we can simply *decide* to believe we can solve a particular problem when no solution is obvious or forthcoming. Changing any belief, whether consciously recognised or not, is one of the hardest things to do. However, armed with a clearer understanding of the real cause of depression we can consider the following steps to help ourselves:

1. Find a way to raise your life-condition. Your *inner life state* has more to do with your ability to believe you can solve your problems than anything that may be going on in your life. If your thoughts are swirling in despair, take action to break free of them and attain a fresh perspective. Become immersed in a great book that moves you, or, watch a movie that transports you. Exercise. Go where it is warm. Chant Nam-myoho-renge-kyo. In short, do what you know from experience bounces your thinking to a more optimistic place.

2. Identify the problem or problems you do not think you can solve. It is amazing how often you don't know why you're depressed and how helpful it can be to figure it out. Making a list of everything that's bothering you—a sort of stream-of-consciousness rant on paper—can be a fantastically helpful exercise. Or if you do know why you're depressed, recognising the cause is

not that you have a problem *per se* but rather that you have a problem *you do not believe you can solve* can be remarkably empowering. Also, sometimes we become depressed not because we have one problem we believe we can't solve but because we have *multiple* problems we believe we cannot solve. Handling challenges can be likened to balancing a "plate" of a certain size: if we pile too many problems onto it, not only do we risk having it topple over, we often find ourselves *wanting* to pitch the whole thing on purpose. When this is the case, allow yourself to only worry about and focus on solving one problem at a time.

3. Identify the reason a problem seems unsolvable. As I pointed out in a previous post, Changing Poison Into Medicine, many things erroneously cause us to conclude we're deadlocked, chief among them our inability to identify a solution to our problem *right now*.

4. Recognize that your mood profoundly influences your thoughts. Once depression has established itself, it takes on a secret life of its own, further diminishing your belief in your ability to solve problems, your ability to plan, and your ability to have hope for the future. In this way the cause of any depression always reinforces itself.

5. Remember that your depressed self is not your true self. Whatever life-condition you find yourself in at any one moment always feels like

the only life-condition you've ever had or will have. But your life-condition can and often does change literally from moment to moment.

Understand that anti-depressants only treat the symptoms of depression. None of the foregoing has been intended as a denial that anti-depressant medication plays a critical role in the treatment of depression. In the right patient, anti-depressants reduce the symptoms of suffering exceptionally well and can be literally life-saving. But they can't make anyone actually *happy* because happiness isn't merely the absence of suffering. The best approach, in my view, is to treat the symptoms of depression with anti-depressants (or cognitive therapy or even electroconvulsive therapy) at the same time you address the underlying cause of the depression itself. I fully recognise that as a means to battle depression—especially a deep, all-consuming depression—these suggestions are inadequate. My point in making them, however, is to emphasise that the single most effective means to resolve a depression is to find a way to tap into our immense power to solve problems.

In a sense, we're all on a journey to find just such a way. For me, the practice of Buddhism has been a consistently effective means by which to win over obstacles I did not believe I could, a tool that has enabled me to manifest wisdom, courage, and most importantly concrete solutions I do not believe I would have stumbled upon had I not been practising. If you have a different means that your experience has demonstrated works, stick with it. If not, spur yourself on to explore other paths until you find one that proves it has real power.

In retrospect, I wish I'd suggested to Mr Burdnt that he think about his guilt over the death of the pedestrian he caused as a problem to be solved— and more importantly as a problem that *could* be solved. Perhaps had I also begun him on an anti-depressant medication to stave off what were obviously strong suicidal thoughts, he might have had time to work through his guilt. Perhaps he could have shaken loose from its grip in time to forgive himself, and his depression might have lifted. But I'll never know. And that is a problem I have to solve for myself.

Let me remind you that as bleak as it may seem, there's always a light at the end of the tunnel. Regardless of your experience, this book will stir up strong emotions. "Pit of Despair" provides deep insight into what it's like to live with depression—insight that will resonate with survivors and help those who aren't afflicted develop a greater understanding of the pain that depression sufferers are going through.

Uroosa Kashif is a writer and a business woman. She is hardworking and has achieved lots of success in business as well as her writing career. She founded the CITS and has expanded her market to Turkey and Singapore too.

WOVEN WORDS

NON-FICTION

www.wovenwordspublishers.com

ISBN 978-93-86897-48-0

9 789386 897480

PROPHETIC

BLINDSPOTS

EDDIE MASSEY III